Little Hands
Learning to Pray

Carine Mackenzie

10 9 8 7 6 5 4 3 2 1
Copyright © 2010 Carine Mackenzie
ISBN 978-1-84550-591-2

Christian Focus Publications
Geanies House, Tain, Ross-shire, IV20 1TW,
Scotland, United Kingdom
www.christianfocus.com
email: info@christianfocus.com

Cover design by Daniel van Straaten
Illustrations by Raffaella Cosco

Printed in China

Written with love for
many children but in particular for
Lydia, Esther and Philip
Lois, Jack, Marianne and Isobel
by their Grandma.

Psalm 128:5

Contents

This book is given to

2017

CONOR JAMES ERSKINE

with love from

GRANNY IRENE + GRANDAD
ROGER.

And this is my prayer: that your love may
abound more and more in knowledge and
depth of insight, so that you may be able
to discern what is best and may be pure and
blameless until the day of Christ.
Philippians 1:9-10

WE LOVE YOU xx

What is Prayer?

It is important to speak to God in prayer. We can speak to him out loud or in our hearts. We can speak to him anywhere and tell him everything. It is helpful to know how other people pray and in the Bible we read many prayers. We can even use these prayers ourselves.

Jesus taught his disciples to pray and we can use that prayer to help us too. In our prayers we tell God that we love him, that we are sorry for what we have done wrong or for the things we have not done that we should have done.

We say thank you to God for all his goodness to us. We can ask him for things that are right and good.

Spot This: Can you find the following pictures as you go through this book?

What do these Words Mean?

Adoration
Meaning: I love you God
We are to pray prayers of worship that tell God that we love him.

Confession
Meaning: I'm sorry God
We are to pray prayers of repentance that tell God we are sorry and that we want to turn away from sin.

Thanksgiving
Meaning: Thank you God
We are to pray prayers of thanks that tell God we are thankful for all that he has done for us and for how wonderful he is.

Supplication
Meaning: Please God

We are to pray prayers of request that tell God what we need or want. He always answers prayer but sometimes he says "Yes," sometimes he says "No," and sometimes he says "Wait".

Adoration
I love you, God

God is in Control

God is in control of
the whole world and
everything in it and all
people. Nothing happens
without his complete
knowledge.

   Job knew this even
when he was having a very hard time. He
lost his crops, animals and even his family.
He became ill and sore. Yet he still prayed to
God. He knew that God was the only one to
help him.

In Your Bible: I know that you can do everything. Job 42:2
Question Time: What did Job lose?
Spot This: Which man has a torn sleeve?

You can be like Job by trusting God when things go wrong.

God is a Rescuer

Isaiah was a prophet to the people of Judah. He spoke God's word to them. He warned them against sin and told them long before about the coming Saviour, the Lord Jesus Christ. He loved to praise God when he thought of all the wonderful things the Lord had done for his people like rescuing them from their enemies.

In Your Bible: O Lord, you are my God . . . you have done marvellous things. Isaiah 25:1

Question Time: What was Isaiah's job?

Spot This: Can you point to two happy faces and two angry faces?

> You can be like Isaiah by remembering all the wonderful things God does for you.

18

God is Worthy

God has made the whole world and everybody in it. He is worthy of praise and worship from every living person. When we offer him praise we can think of how wonderful he is – God never changes. He deserves to be praised. He is worth it.

In Your Bible: Let the people praise you, O God; Let all the peoples praise you. Psalm 67:5
Question Time: Can you name something that God never does?
Spot This: Where is the moon in the picture?

You can praise God by counting all the good things he has done for you.

20

God is Great

David loved to praise God. He composed many songs of praise called Psalms. Some he composed when he was a shepherd boy working outside with the sheep. Others he sang when he was a soldier and a king, afraid of his enemies. He remembered how great God was, the king of the whole earth.

✋ **In Your Bible: O Lord, our Lord, how majestic is your name in all the earth. Psalm 8:1**

Question Time: What did David write?

Spot this: Where is David's harp in the picture?

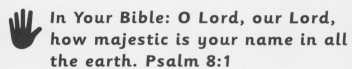

You can be like David and write about how great God is.

22

God is Strong

David spoke this prayer when he was saved by God from his enemy Saul who was trying to hurt him. We can tell God that we love him because he loved us first. He has given us everything we have – even our life.

In Your Bible: I will love you, O Lord, my strength. Psalm 18:1

Question Time: Who was David's enemy?

Spot This: How many trees can you see in this picture?

You can be like David by praying to God when you *feel* afraid.

24

God is a Helper

Moses led the children of Israel out of Egypt where they were slaves. God helped them all the way. Miraculously God caused the Red Sea to part, making a path for the people to cross safely. Pharaoh's army was destroyed in the Red Sea as they chased after the Israelites to recapture them. Moses composed a song of praise to God who had delivered him and the people from their miserable life in Egypt. Moses and the people sang together . . . "The Lord is my strength and my song . . ."

In Your Bible: The Lord is my strength and my song. Exodus 15:2

Question Time: What miracle did God do at the Red Sea?

Spot This: What can you see in the water?

You can be like Moses by remembering to thank God.

Confession
I am Sorry, God

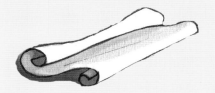

God Forgives

God wants us to be truly sorry for our sins and to turn from them to himself. If we realise that we are sinners and tell God that we know we are sinners and that we are really sorry, then the faithful and just and loving God will forgive our sins because his Son, Jesus Christ, has died on the cross to take the punishment due to us. This is a wonderful gift that we do not deserve.

In Your Bible: If we confess our sins, God is faithful and just and will forgive us our sins.
1 John 1:9
Question Time: Who died on the cross to take the punishment of sin?
Spot This: What are the boys fighting over?

You can be forgiven if you trust in Jesus Christ, God's Son.

God Listens

Daniel was taken away from his home by cruel men. They took him to the far away land of Babylon. There he worshipped and served God. He knew that God was in control. He prayed to God often. He prayed to God not just for himself but for the other people of Israel living in Babylon with him. He confessed that they had all sinned and begged God to forgive and to listen to his prayer and allow the people of Israel back to Jerusalem again.

In Your Bible: O Lord, hear! O Lord forgive; O Lord, listen and act. Daniel 9:19

Question Time: What far away land was Daniel taken to?

Spot This: How many palm trees can you see in this picture?

You can be like Daniel by praying for other people.

God Cleanses

King David had done something
very bad. He knew that he
had sinned. He asked God to
forgive him. He knew that only
God could wash away his sin. Then he would
be clean again; so clean in God's sight – even
whiter than snow. He prayed that God would
wash away his sin.

**In Your Bible: Wash me, and
I shall be whiter than snow.
Psalm 51:7
Question Time: What did David
need washed away?**
**Spot This: How many buttons has the
snowman got on his chest?**

> You can be whiter
> than snow in God's
> sight when you say
> sorry to him for your
> sin and ask him to
> wash your sin away.

God Punishes

David ordered Joab, the captain of his army to count all the people in the land. Joab thought this was a bad idea, but David insisted, so Joab obeyed.

David eventually realised that God was not pleased with what he had done. His kingdom was powerful because of God not because of how many people lived there. David confessed his sin to God. He knew he had done a foolish thing, which God punished. David offered sacrifices to God to show how sorry he was.

In Your Bible: David said, "Lord, take away the guilt of your servant. I have done a very foolish thing." 2 Samuel 24:10
Question Time: Was David's idea good?
Spot This: How many pieces of paper can you see in this picture?

God punishes sin but he also forgives and forgets when we are truly sorry.

God is Merciful

Jesus told a story of two men who went to the temple to pray.

One man was very pleased with himself and told God how good he was.

The other, a tax-collector, bowed his head humbly and prayed, "God, have mercy on me, a sinner."

God wants us to pray like that man.

In Your Bible: The tax-collector prayed, "God, have mercy on me, a sinner." Luke 18:13

Question Time: What was the job of the man who prayed for mercy?

Spot This: Can you point to all the jewellery in this picture?

> Don't be like the proud man. Don't tell God how good you are. Everyone has sinned and needs God's forgiveness.

God is to be Worshipped

Solomon was wise and wealthy. He made a beautiful temple to be the house of worship of God.

Thousands of workers built the temple and decorated it with gold and jewels. After seven years it was finished at last. Then the priests carried in the golden chest holding God's holy laws. Solomon prayed at the dedication of the temple. He thanked God but he also confessed to God the sin of the people and asked God to forgive.

In Your Bible: Solomon said, "We have sinned, we have done wrong, we have acted wickedly."
1 Kings 8:47
Question Time: How long did it take to build the temple?
Spot This: What two colours are on the fan?

We should keep the Lord's Day as a special day to worship God.

Thanksgiving
Thank you, God

God is Glorious

David wanted to build a temple where God would be worshipped but he had been a man of war, God did not allow that. His son, Solomon, who reigned in a time of peace, was given that honour. David gathered together gold, silver, bronze, iron, wood and precious stones and other building materials. David knew that his son would carry out the work and he was glad. He praised God and thanked him for all his goodness.

 In Your Bible: Now, God, we give you thanks, and praise your glorious name. 1 Chronicles 29:13 Question Time: Can you list the items that David gathered together for the temple?
Spot This: In the picture can you point to the older man and then to the younger man?

Think of all the great and good words that you can - these describe God.

God is Good

God is always good. Everything that he does is good. When he made the world, he knew that it was good. We should thank him for the beautiful world he has given us — with water, food, shelter, family and friends.

God is so good that he gave his son, Jesus Christ, to be the one and only Saviour of sinners. How thankful we should be.

In Your Bible: O give thanks to the Lord for he is good. Psalm 107:1
Question Time: What is the name of the one and only Saviour?
Spot This: Can you see where the cookies are in the picture?

Are you sorry for your sin? Are you thankful for Jesus the one and only Saviour?

God Gives a Gift

Some things are so amazing it can be difficult to describe them. God's gifts are like that. He gave us his Son the Lord Jesus Christ to be our Saviour. There is no gift more wonderful.

 In Your Bible: Thanks be to God for his indescribable gift. 2 Corinthians 9:15

Question Time: What gift did God give?

Spot This: Is the girl in a low building or a high building?

> Getting a gift that you don't deserve is amazing. Sinners don't deserve God's forgiveness but he is still forgiving.

God Gives Many Gifts

Everything we have comes from God. He gives us our breath and our life. He gives us food and drink. He gives us friends and family. He gives us eyes to see and ears to hear. For all these gifts and thousands more, we should say "Thank you."

In Your Bible: Always giving thanks to God the Father for everything, in the name of our Lord Jesus Christ. Ephesians 5:20
Question Time: What parts of your body can you use to help others?
Spot This: Can you spot where the caterpillar is?

Think of a new thing every day to thank God for.

God Should be Thanked

Ten lepers met Jesus one day. Leprosy is a serious skin disease. They all asked Jesus to have mercy on them and help them.

Jesus healed them. They had to go to the priest. He told them for sure that the disease was gone. They could return to their homes.

Only one remembered to come back to Jesus and say thank you.

 In Your Bible: He threw himself at Jesus' feet and thanked him. Luke 17:16

Question: How many lepers were there?

Spot This: Can you find a leper who is wearing shoes in the picture?

> **When God helps you, do you remember to say thank you to him?**

God Gives Wisdom

Daniel loved the Lord God. He served the King of Babylon. The king had a troubling dream. No one could tell him what it meant. But during the night God revealed the meaning of the dream to Daniel. Daniel praised God, "Praise be to the name of God forever and ever. Wisdom and power are his."

Daniel was able to tell the king the meaning of the dream. He knew that God had given him this special wisdom and he was thankful.

 In Your Bible: I thank and praise you, O God. You have given me wisdom. Daniel 2:23
Question Time: Who did Daniel love?
Spot This: What animal has been carved onto the king's throne?

You can be like Daniel. Be thankful to God for the things you can do.

Supplication
Please God

Jesus Helps

A lady came to Jesus one day, crying out to him to heal her daughter. Her daughter was very sick and troubled. Jesus' friends wanted to send her away.

She knelt down before Jesus and said, "Lord, help me."

Jesus did help her.

Her daughter was better right away.

In Your Bible: Lord, help me. Matthew 15:25

Question Time: Who wanted to send the lady away?

Spot This: What colour is the girl's head scarf?

When you need help, pray to Jesus immediately.

Jesus Rescues

Jesus was in a boat with his friends when a big storm blew up on the lake. Jesus was asleep. The waves lashed into the boat. The friends were scared. They woke Jesus up, saying, "Lord, save us."

Jesus got up and told the wind and the waves to be still. There was a complete calm. The friends were amazed.

In Your Bible: Lord, save us. Matthew 8:25

Question Time: What was Jesus doing in the boat when the storm started?

Spot This: Can you point to the lightning?

Jesus is Merciful

Blind Bartimaeus sat by the road
begging. When he heard that
Jesus was coming, he shouted
out, "Jesus, have mercy on me."

People told him to be quiet but he shouted
all the more.

Jesus called him over. "What do you
want?"

"I want to see," he replied.

Jesus immediately healed him.

**In Your Bible: Jesus, have mercy
on me. Mark 10:47**

**Question Time: What did the
people say to the blind beggar?**

**Spot This: What does Bartimaeus have
in his hand?**

**You can trust in God.
He has power over our bodies.**

Jesus is the Saviour

Jesus was put to death on a cross of wood. Two men were crucified at the same time. One was sorry for his sin and realised that Jesus was the Son of God.

"Remember me," he said to Jesus, "when you come into your kingdom."

Jesus gave him more than he asked for. "Today you will be with me in paradise," he said.

In Your Bible: The Lord remembers us and will bless us. Psalm 115:12

Question Time: What was the cross made out of?

Spot This: How many nails can you see?

God often gives more than we ask for. The Bible tells us that heaven is going to be even better than we can imagine!

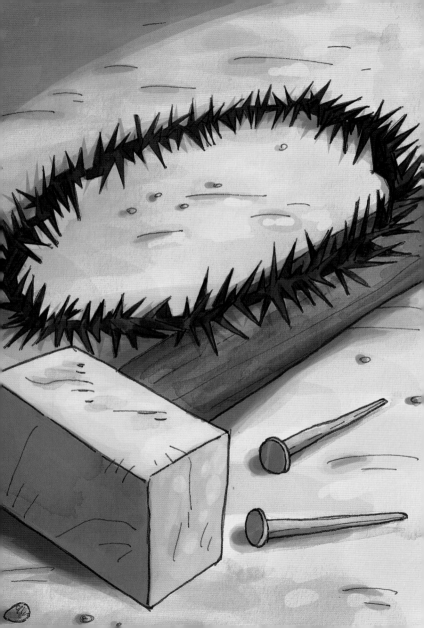

God's Word
Teaches us How to Pray

God's Ways are Best

It is God's Word that teaches us about how to pray to God. God tells us in his Word, the Bible, how we should live. His ways are best. If we live to please him, we will be blessed.

Jesus described himself as the Way. This is because the only way to come to God is by trusting and following Jesus, his Son.

 In Your Bible: Show me your ways, O Lord, teach me your paths. Psalm 25:9.

Question Time: Whose ways are best?

Spot This: How many signs are there in this picture?

To be blessed means to be made truly happy and joyful by God.

God Wants to Help Us

When we read the Bible, we do not always understand it. It is good to pray to the Lord before we read and ask him to make it easy for us, and help us to understand.

God wants us to ask him for his help.

In Your Bible: Open my eyes that I may see wonderful things in your law. Psalm 119:18

Question Time: What should we do before we read the Bible?

Spot This: Can you find a square toy and a round toy?

Read your Bible and pray every day. You need to do this.

Secret Prayer

Jesus tells us to pray to God in secret, in a private place. We can pray in our heart and no one else need know that we are praying. God hears our prayer even when no one else does.

In Your Bible: When you pray, go into your room, close the door and pray to your Father in secret. And your Father who sees in secret shall reward you openly. Matthew 6:6

Question: Who always hears our prayers?

Spot This: How did the boy get up the tree?

You can pray anywhere at all. God is always listening.

Do Not Give Up

Jesus told the story about a woman who kept coming to the judge to ask for justice. This judge did not care about doing the right thing but because the woman kept on asking, he eventually said, "I had better do as she asks because I am getting sick and tired of her coming so often."

Even an unjust judge answers continual pleas for help. Our gracious God is much more likely to answer our continued prayers than an unjust judge is.

 In Your Bible: Men ought always to pray and not give up. Luke 18:1
Question: What did the woman keep on doing?
Spot This: Who is looking cross in this picture?

Keep praying to God. Don't give up. He loves to hear and answer prayer.

74

Pray About Everything

We can pray about everything
– ask God to forgive the bad
things we do; tell him when
we feel sad; thank him for all
his goodness to us; ask him for
help and guidance; tell him about our friends
and family; tell him when we feel happy
and praise him for being a great God, and
sending the Lord Jesus Christ, his Son, to die
for our sins.

In Your Bible: In everything by prayers and supplications with thanksgiving let your requests be made known to God. Philippians 4:6
Question: Can you remember one thing that we can pray to God about?
Spot This: Can you point to the things in the picture that you drink, and then to the things that you eat?

You can bring all your troubles to God.
You can pray to him about everything.

Pray Anywhere

You do not need to be in a church to pray. You can pray everywhere and anywhere. You can pray in the playground, at the bus stop, in the car, in the kitchen. You can pray in your home, on holiday even on the other side of the world.

In Your Bible: I want men everywhere to lift up holy hands in prayer. 1 Timothy 2:8
Question: Where can you pray?
Spot This: How many doors can you see on the plane?

Think about all the different places you can pray. Have you prayed today?

Pray Through Christ's Name

The name of Jesus Christ shows that he is Saviour, the special one sent from God to deliver his people from sin.

   Jesus is God and man. He is the link between God and us. When we pray "in the name of Jesus Christ" we are asking God to hear us because of what Jesus has done. He died and he rose again for us.

In Your Bible: I will do whatever you ask in my name, so that the Son may bring glory to the Father.
John 14:13
Question: What did Jesus do for his people?
Spot This: How many pieces of chalk can you see in the picture?

When you pray - remember you are praying to God, your Heavenly Father.

Pray Without Stopping

We should always be ready and willing to pray. We do not say, "I only pray at bedtime," or "I only pray before I eat my food," or "I can only pray in church."

God wants to hear us praying to him always.

In Your Bible: Pray without ceasing. 1 Thessalonians 5:17
Question: At what times can you pray to God?
Spot This: Point to the person who is carrying something in this picture.

You can pray to God at anytime, in any place and about anything.

The Lord's Prayer

The disciples asked Jesus
to teach them to pray. He
answered them by saying, "Pray like this:

Our Father in heaven, hallowed be your
name, your kingdom come, your will be done
on earth as it is in heaven.

Give us this day our daily bread.

Forgive us our sins as we forgive those
who sin against us.

Do not lead us into temptation but
deliver us from the evil one, for yours is the
kingdom, and the power, and the glory.
Amen."

**In Your Bible: Teach us to pray.
Luke 11:1**

**Question: Who asked Jesus to
teach them to pray?**
**Spot This: Count how many glasses of
water there are on the table.**

**This is a prayer for us to say. Jesus
wants us to pray to God our Father.**

Praying for other Christians

Christians belong to a family —
the family of God. They should
love and take care of each
other. One of the best things
they can do is pray for others
who trust in the Lord Jesus.

Some people who are Christians suffer greatly
because they believe in Jesus and follow his
commands. Even though we do not know these
people we can still pray for them and ask God
to keep them faithful and strong.

 **In Your Bible: Be alert and always
keep on praying for all the saints.
Ephesians 6:18**
**Question: What family do Christians
belong to?**
**Spot This: Can you see the country
where you live on the map?**

> **Pray for Christians at home and
> throughout the world.**

Jesus Prayed

Jesus Prayed for Others

Just before Jesus died he prayed to his Father for his disciples. He knew he was going to leave them. He asked God to look  after them and that they would be united with each other. He prayed that God's truth would make them pure and holy. Jesus also prayed for all who would believe in him — even for those who trust in him today.

In Your Bible: Holy Father, protect them by the power of your name—the name you gave me—so that they may be one as we are one. John 17:11
Question: Who did Jesus pray to?
Spot This: Can you find the door and all the windows in this picture?

Jesus prayed for all the people who would one day love and follow him.

Jesus in Gethsemane

Jesus went to the Garden of Gethsemane to pray. He knew that he was facing death soon. He was very sad. His disciples came too but soon fell asleep, even though Jesus asked them to watch.

Jesus prayed to his Father for himself, "If it is at all possible, don't let me go through this suffering."

Jesus knew that God's plan had to be worked out for his glory. "Not what I will," he prayed, "but what you will."

In Your Bible: Not what I will, but what you will. Mark 14:36
Question: What did the disciples do?
Spot This: Can you point out which two disciples are yawning?

> **Jesus prayed that God would do what he wanted to do. So should we.**

Jesus Prayed At the Cross

It is easy to pray for our friends and for people who are nice to us. But Jesus prayed for soldiers who were treating him so cruelly, hammering nails into his hands and feet. They were obeying orders from their masters. Jesus asked God to forgive them. They did not really understand what they were doing.

God's mercy is so amazing that he can save the worst of sinners.

 In Your Bible: Father, forgive them for they do not know what they do. Luke 23:34

Question: What did the soldiers do to Jesus?

Spot This: What is in one of the the centurion's hands?

Jesus prayed for his enemies. We should pray for those who are horrible to us.

Jesus Gave Thanks

A big crowd of people came to hear Jesus teach. They were far from home and shops. One boy had a picnic of five loaves and two fish. Jesus gave thanks for this food before he divided it up and multiplied it, making it enough to feed the whole crowd of people – more than 5,000.

We should remember to say thank you for our food. God gives it all to us.

In Your Bible: Jesus then took the loaves, gave thanks, and distributed to those who were seated as much as they wanted. He did the same with the fish. John 6:11
Question: How many loaves did the little boy have in his picnic?
Spot This: Can you find the boy who has a fish in his hands?

Thank God for food and drink. Pray for those who do not have enough to eat.

Jesus Prayed at His Baptism

Jesus prayed at the important occasion of his baptism. Jesus had no sin, so his baptism was not a symbol of sin being washed  away. He wanted to be baptised to show that although he was God indeed, he was also a man. God, the Holy Spirit, came down like a dove and God the Father spoke from heaven, "This is my Son, whom I love; with him I am well pleased."

In Your Bible: And as he was praying, heaven was opened and the Holy Spirit descended on him in bodily form like a dove. Luke 3:21
Question: What did Jesus not have?
Spot This: How many trees can you see in this picture?

God himself said that he was very pleased with Jesus. We should be too.

Jesus Prayed All Night

Before Jesus appointed his twelve disciples he spent the whole night praying to God his Father. God never goes to sleep. If we waken up in the night, we can pray to him and know that he can see us in the dark and hear us in the night.

In Your Bible: Jesus ... spent the night praying to God. Luke 6:12
Question: What does God never do?
Spot This: What shape is on the girl's blanket?

We can do what Jesus did and pray during the night.

Jesus Prayed Early

Jesus sometimes got up very early and went to a quiet place to pray. He could be alone there speaking to God without disturbance from others. His friends came looking for him.

"People are looking for you," they said. Jesus went round the country preaching the gospel which is the good news about Jesus and the forgiveness of sins.

In Your Bible: Very early in the morning... Jesus got up, left the house and went off to a solitary place where he prayed. Mark 1:35
Question: What is the Gospel?
Spot This: Can you point to the dark blue scarf?

We can follow the example of Jesus and pray every morning.

Bible People
Who Prayed

Daniel's Prayer

Daniel prayed to God often.
Three times a day he got down
on his knees and prayed and
thanked God. Daniel prayed
for himself and for his people,
the Jews, who were in trouble.
Even when the king gave orders
that no one should pray to God,
Daniel still did what was right
and prayed to his God as before.

**In Your Bible: Three times a day
he got down on his knees and
prayed, giving thanks to his God.**
Daniel 6:10
Question: Who did Daniel pray for?
**Spot This: Can you find another picture
like this in the book? How does Daniel
look different in this picture?**

**We should be like Daniel and pray to
God every day.**

Hannah's Prayer

Hannah really wanted to
have a baby boy. She kept
on praying to God about it.
God answered her prayer and
Samuel was born. Hannah was delighted.
When Samuel was old enough, Hannah gave
him to the Lord God to work for him in
the house of God. Hannah was happy and
praised God.

**In Your Bible: My heart rejoices in
the Lord. 1 Samuel 2:1**
Question: Where did Samuel work?
**Spot This: Point to the littlest person in
the picture and then point to the oldest
person.**

> **Keep on praying
> to God. He always
> listens ... and
> remember that Jesus
> is praying for his
> people too.**

Nehemiah's Prayer

Nehemiah was far away from his home town Jerusalem. He heard that the walls of the town were broken and the gates burned down. Nehemiah wanted to go back to build the walls again. He prayed to God about it for days. He asked God to help him as he asked for permission to go back to Jerusalem. The permission was granted and Nehemiah rebuilt the walls, with God's help.

 In Your Bible: Listen to my prayer, O Lord. Give me success. Nehemiah 1:11

Question: What did Nehemiah want to build?

Spot This: Can you find the ladder?

God listens to your request for help even when you are far away from home.

Jabez' Prayer

Jabez prayed to God for blessing on his life. He knew he needed God to keep him from harm and pain. His name means "Distress". We do not know any details about Jabez' life, but we know that God granted him his request.

In Your Bible: Oh, that you would bless me and enlarge my territory. Let your hand be with me and keep me from harm, so that I will be free from pain. 1 Chronicles 4:10
Question: What did Jabez' name mean?
Spot This: Can you find things that you could eat in this picture?

The greatest blessing God has given us is his Son, Jesus Christ.

Elijah's Prayer

Elijah had a contest with prophets who worshipped a false god. Elijah wanted to prove that the Lord was the true God. The true powerful God would send fire to burn up an offering on the altar. When Elijah prayed, God heard and answered. Fire came down from heaven and burnt up the offering and the altar. The people knew that the Lord was indeed God.

In Your Bible: Answer me, O Lord, answer me so that these people will know that you, O Lord are God. 1 Kings 18:37

Question: What did God send down from heaven?

Spot This: Point to something that you could carry water in.

We know that God is the true God because he kept his word and sent his Son - the true Saviour.

Solomon's Prayer

Solomon was a wise and wealthy king, the son of David. Solomon lived in a beautiful palace, but wanted to build a lovely temple, a house for the Lord. It took seven years to build this temple using cut stone, cedar wood, gold and wonderful furnishings. When all was ready, Solomon dedicated the temple to the Lord. He prayed to God for his blessing and forgiveness.

✋ **In Your Bible: Hear from heaven, your dwelling place, and when you hear, forgive. 1 Kings 8:30**
Question: How many years did it take to build the temple?
Spot This: Who is wearing a crown?

We should be like Solomon and pray to God for forgiveness of our sins.

Paul and Silas in Prison

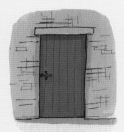

Paul and Silas were thrown in prison. They were accused of causing a disturbance but it wasn't their fault. The jailer tied them up. But Paul and Silas prayed and sang to God.

Suddenly an earthquake shook the building and everyone's chains were loosed. The jailer was alarmed but Paul assured him that all the prisoners were still there. The jailor asked how he could be saved. That night he believed in the Lord Jesus Christ.

In Your Bible: Believe in the Lord Jesus, and you will be saved—you and your household. Acts 16:31

Question: What were Paul and Silas doing at midnight?

Spot This: Can you see a spear in this picture?

You can be like Paul and Silas who praised God even when things were bad.

God Listens
To Our Prayers

God Answers Prayer

If a little boy asks his father for an egg, of course his father loves to give him one. If he asked for bread, his father would not give him a stone. Jesus tells us that if a human father wants to give good gifts to his children, how much more will our Heavenly Father give good things to those who ask him.

In Your Bible: Ask and it shall be given you. Matthew 7:7
Question: Who gives us good gifts when we ask him?
Spot This: What other things are beside the spoon in this picture?

Jesus knows how loving and full of mercy his Father is to us. We can trust what Jesus says about God the Father.

Christ Prays for His People

 Jesus died but rose again from the dead. He ascended up through the clouds into heaven. Jesus is in heaven and is now praying for his people here on earth. We may forget to pray for a friend but Jesus never forgets.

In Your Bible: Christ ever lives to make intercession. Hebrews 7:25
Question: Where is Jesus now?
Spot This: Can you point to what was used as the door on Jesus' tomb?

Jesus speaks to God the Father on our behalf. God never forgets his people.

Praying Together

The church is made up of all the people who trust in the Lord Jesus. The church meets together to pray.

When Peter was in prison, his friends in the church prayed for his release. They could hardly believe when their prayers were answered and Peter arrived at the door.

 In Your Bible: The church was earnestly praying to God. Acts 12:5

Question: Why were Peter's friends surprised?

Spot This: What time of day is it in the picture?

You can be like the humble man by asking Jesus to save you.

Singing a Prayer

A prayer can be words spoken out loud. We can also sing a prayer to God. David sang many prayers to God – some of these are called psalms. David told God how glad he was that the Lord was his shepherd, caring for him and leading him. We can use this psalm as a prayer too.

In Your Bible: The Lord is my Shepherd. Psalm 23

Question: What is the special name for a prayer that you sing?

Spot This: Who has long hair and who has short hair in this picture?

Jesus is the Good Shepherd. He truly takes care of us like no one else can.

God Hears Silent Words

We can pray without even saying the words out loud. A lady who had been ill for many years saw Jesus in a crowd of people. As she edged closer, she thought to herself, "If I can just touch the hem of his clothes, I will be healed." She did manage to touch Jesus' clothes and her silent prayer was answered.

In Your Bible: Daughter your faith has healed you. Go in peace and be free from your suffering.
Mark 5:34
Question: What did the sick lady touch?
Spot This: How many legs can you see in this picture?

You can be like the sick lady. Bring your troubles to Jesus and he will hear you.

Prayers of Little Children

God loves to hear little children praying. When Jesus went to the temple at Jerusalem the children called out to him in praise, "Hosanna to the Son of David."

Some of the officials were annoyed but Jesus reminded them of a verse in Psalm Eight. "Praise to God comes from the mouths of infants and babies."

God hears the prayer and praise of a very little child.

In Your Bible: Out of the mouths of babes and nursing infants you have perfected praise. Matthew 21:16
Question: What psalm did Jesus remind the officials of?
Spot This: How many pillars can you see?

You are a child - God listens to your prayers too. How wonderful!

BIBLE PASSAGES

1. Job 42:2
2. Isaiah 25:1
3. Psalm 67:5
4. Psalm 8:1
5. Psalm 18:1
6. Exodus 15:2
7. 1 John 1:9
8. Daniel 9:19
9. Psalm 51:7
10. 2 Samuel 24:10
11. Luke 18:13
12. 1 Kings 8:47
13. 1 Chronicles 29:13
14. Psalm 107:1
15. 2 Corinthians 9:15
16. Ephesians 5:20
17. Luke 17:16
18. Daniel 2:23
19. Matthew 15:25
20. Matthew 8:25
21. Mark 10:47
22. Psalm 115:12
23. Psalm 25:9
24. Psalm 119:18
25. Matthew 6:6
26. Luke 18:1

Can you remember how God helped these people?

Paul and Silas

David

Daniel

The Sick Woman

Can you remember why these people prayed to God?

Jabez

Moses

Solomon

Hannah

My Prayer Diary:

Every day:
Tell God how wonderful he is. Ask forgiveness for your sin. Thank him for looking after you. Ask him for help and protection during the day and the night. Pray about tomorrow.

Monday
Pray for your family. Thank God for the people who care for you. Ask God to help them. Thank God that he is your Heavenly Father and that all who trust him are his children.

Tuesday
Pray for your friends. Ask God to help you love and care for them. Thank God for Jesus who is the closest and best friend anyone can have.

Wednesday
Ask God to help your teachers to do their jobs. Thank God for giving you people who want to help you to learn.

Thursday

Pray for people who look after your country such as nurses, doctors, soldiers, people in Government and the Police. Ask God to help them as they do their jobs. Pray that God will bring many of these people to trust in him.

Friday

Pray for people who live in other countries around the world where they do not have enough to eat. Ask God to help and comfort them.

Saturday

Pray to God about what is going to happen next week. Ask God to help you not to disobey him and to love him more and more.

Sunday

Pray for the people in your church. Ask God to help all those who teach his Word. Ask God to give your pastor strength and understanding so that he can show you the truth of God's Word, the Bible.

Meet the Author:
Carine Mackenzie

How can a basin of water help you write your first book? Carine Mackenzie wrote her first book, *Gideon - Soldier of God*, in the kitchen of her home in Inverness, Scotland. A two year old was at her feet playing blissfully with a basin of water.

"It was the only way I could be sure of getting some peace and quiet to get on with it ... and it worked."

The two year old is now married with a growing family of her own and Carine's first attempt at writing has grown too. Her talent for retelling Bible stories has meant that children from all over the world have been given the opportunity to discover Jesus Christ for themselves. The first title written in the kitchen with the assistance of a basin of water has inspired the production of many other books and Carine now has over fifty different titles in print and sales of over three million books.

Also by Carine Mackenzie

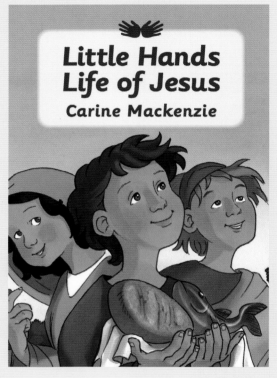

The life of Jesus is a story that will never end. His story
is an adventure that you can join. It's a mystery that
you can solve and it's a love story that's about you,
God and his great, loving, wonderful heart; a heart
that beats with a never-ending love for his people.

ISBN: 978-1-84550-339-0

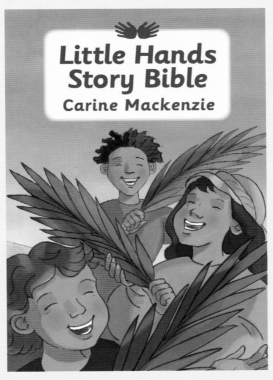

Little Hands Story Bible
Carine Mackenzie

There is a story that runs throughout the whole Bible.
It's one that will never end and that you can be a part
of. It's a story of love, and sometimes of sadness, but
ultimately it's a story of hope. A hope that you can
share.

ISBN: 978-1-84550-435-9

CHRISTIAN FOCUS PUBLICATIONS

Christian Focus · Christian Heritage · CF4K · Mentor

Christian Focus Publications publishes books for adults and children under its four main imprints: Christian Focus, CF4K, Mentor and Christian Heritage. Our books reflect that God's word is reliable and Jesus is the way to know him, and live for ever with him.

Our children's publication list includes a Sunday School curriculum that covers pre-school to early teens; puzzle and activity books. We also publish personal and family devotional titles, biographies and inspirational stories that children will love.

If you are looking for quality Bible teaching for children then we have an excellent range of Bible story and age specific theological books.

From pre-school to teenage fiction, we have it covered!

Find us at our web page:
www.christianfocus.com

CF4•K
Because you're never too young to know Jesus